All
of *Us*

First published in 2018 by Landing Press

Landing Press
landingpressnz@gmail.com
www.landingpress.wordpress.com

A catalogue record for this book is available from the National Library of New Zealand.
ISBN 978-0-473-45168-4

Printed by Ligare
Cover design by Rowan Heap and carina gallegos

This book was taken from manuscript to bookshelf by students of the Whitireia New Zealand publishing programme, who worked on the editing, production, design, publicity, and marketing. For more information about our editing and publishing training, visit www.whitireiapublishing.co.nz

All of Us

ADRIENNE JANSEN   CARINA GALLEGOS

Dedication

To the people who've made the journey, thank you for the conversations, and for giving us a window into your world.

Contents

Where did these poems come from?

Adrienne: I wanted to write a series of poems from two perspectives: what does someone from Syria, for example, experience when they go to a railway station, compared to what I experience going to a railway station? What would happen if we each wrote about our experience of the railway station?

So I started to write a series of poems that were about 'there' and 'here'. One of the reasons it appealed to me was because I didn't want to take on the voice of the migrant or refugee. I might be recording the stories and experiences they've told me, but I'm not taking on their voice.

Now you can talk about where your poems came from.

carina: my poems aren't imagined either, they're just sharing the experiences that people have shared with me. they're the observations of 'here' and 'there'. when you work with people or communities from refugee backgrounds, you hear these stories over and over again. the stories go on for days and people experience them in their heads every day, and to tell them in a poetic context brings them alive in a more succinct way. but we don't get to experience the 'there', we only experience the 'here'.

coming from a migrant background it was easy for me to relate to some of their stories too.

Adrienne: Both of us are retelling the stories that we've heard and heard and which we think are very important to pass on, and in this case, we're recording them in poetry.

carina: exactly. it's storytelling poetry.

that was the other part of the vision – that we were going to write poetry that was accessible to a wide range of people. it wasn't conceptual poetry, it wasn't difficult, it was poetry that people could read and understand, even if there were other layers of meaning, even if there were stories between the lines. there was something there, regardless of whether you could read between the lines or not.

Adrienne: Tell me why you don't use capital letters.

carina: because i don't like capital letters.

Adrienne: Because … ?

carina: ever since i was a little girl i've had an issue with authority (that's a longer conversation). i don't mean for the lack of capital letters to be an obstacle for people. it's quite common for poets to play with capital letters and punctuation and with the aesthetics of letters and words. i love full stops and commas and use them in a very traditional way. i just don't like capital letters. i don't even use them to spell my name.

Adrienne: So that was a challenge for us, how to combine two quite different styles. I use capitals and punctuation because I see them as a kind of small signpost to the reader and a kind of fine-tuning for the writer. That would be my approach.

But there are other differences in style too. Like yours – would you describe your style as Latin American style? It's more discursive.

carina: we talk a lot. latin americans, i mean.

Adrienne: You talk a lot. Right. And of course, New Zealanders don't talk so much. This could be very interesting!

carina: we're long-winded people.

Adrienne: That's why you've got longer poems than mine. We're both being true to type.

carina: and there's also the weather factor. we've been told that in the poems it rains a lot. the weather here is not tropical. if we lived in central america or south america, we'd be writing about mugginess or bad hair days. but in new zealand the challenge is the weather, even for people who were born here. it's the cold weather that challenges people.

Adrienne: So that's why it rains a lot.

carina: that's why it rains a lot.

Adrienne: In the poems.

carina: because in new zealand it rains a lot.

all of us

once upon a time
all of us here
were one of them there.

maybe
in another skin
in a life before.
maybe
only a few weeks ago.

land of the long white cloud,
land of no borders,
floating
adrift
near the end of the world,
near the end of the sea.

we came
and stayed
and with our accents
call
this place
home.

homework

she waits
for her children
to fall asleep
before she opens
their schoolbags
and studies their homework.
they learn
so much faster
and she's falling behind.
they speak her language
with an accent now
and she can't
understand what they say
when they speak
among themselves
in their new
mother tongue.

Lost in translation

Lev has learnt
the word in English.
Rabbit.

He points at the book
and says in his thick accent
'Rabbit.'

It's freezing cold,
frost on the window.
'Rabbit' comes out
in a rush of smoke.

'No' I say,
'that's not a rabbit.'
I point at the book.
'It's a pig.'

He breathes heavily,
clouds of white steam
rising around him.
He goes to the window.
A dog is running
on the white grass.
'Rabbit!' he shouts
'Rabbit! Rabbit! Rabbit!'
and bursts into tears.

read

'it says here'
the man in blue
points to a trail
like black ants
lined up on paper,
'that you can read.'

both men
stare
at each other.

'so'
asks the man in blue again,
'can you read?'

'of course' luis says.
he rests his elbows on
his knobbly knees
as he leans forward,
the chair too big
for his small brown limbs.

he can read tropical rainforests,
the medicinal use
of *yoco lianas*,
the magic that lives
inside the *yagé*.

he can read the notes
in the song of the *tangará*,
the silence between
one gust of wind and another.

he can read
her adobe brown face,
the space between her brows,
the creases of her mouth,
the furrows
in the corners of her eyes.

'what does it say here?'
the man in blue
points
to the trail of ants
again.

'i don't know'
luis replies.
'the ants
on your page
don't speak
to me.'

english

'it's a big jigsaw puzzle'
the woman tells me.

she spreads her arms wide
above her head.
'it's a big big puzzle
with hundreds,
no, thousands
of pieces
about this size'
– her thumb and index finger
grow two centimetres apart –
'and some are even smaller.'

'the teacher is patient.
she tries to teach us
how to put this puzzle together.'
the woman stops and laughs.
'but we don't know
what the puzzle looks like.
how can we make a picture
we know nothing of?'

another shakes her head.
she is tired.
'english is
like a big big country.
we don't have a map
and we did not choose it
but it is
the last country
left in the world.'

Writing in Arabic

Ishtar pauses, lifts the pen,
and stares through the tall window
at the light sinking behind the hills,
the darkness rising from the earth,
and I think she is dreaming of
the mountains behind Alqosh.
But then she says 'My head is becoming a sieve.
I hardly remember how to write my name.'

Mary

You smacked her for talking
in her own language.
You made her language a sin.

You stole her words, changed them
and made them your own.
But they're not.

Now they are no one's.
They are skin with no bones,
leaves with no branch.

Listen, all of you, to her name.
It is strange and beautiful.
It means golden fruit.

'No' you say,
'I will not call her by that name.
I will call her Mary.'

hearing aid

the teacher
speaks loudly
to juan
in english.
he wonders
if she thinks
he can't hear her.

juan
speaks loudly
back to her
in spanish.
she wonders
if he thinks
she can't hear him.

The English class

1.
Every week, Phoeun brings lettuces,
a handful of parsley, or new white garlic.

They're payment for two struggling hours
of copying strange shapes onto paper,
twisting the mouth around a sound
which leaps away just when she thinks she's got it.

But sometimes there's a moment when
a sound becomes a meaning
one can fix into the mind,
like hanging a small picture on a wall.

'Did you grow this lettuce, Phoeun?'
'Yes, I grow it.'

Ah!

2.
Sim
receives each page
I pass him
hands together
head bowed
like a gift.

3.
Khieng has a lurex blouse,
a purple Thai skirt
and an orange shopping bag.
A tropical flower plucked
from a noisy crowded market

and dropped into a silent
grey street of state houses.

4.
Thet is lying on the floor.
Aung is talking about her father
and memory has felled him.

5.
There is a photo
of a golden Buddha.
'What's the word?' I ask.
'God' one replies.
'Buddha' says Phalla
and writes it in Khmer.

'How do you say it?' I ask.
'Preahpout.'
But I've no way
to write that open o,
the way the jaw drops down
to let the spirit jump out
from the throat.

6.
Every day Noen comes to the
doorway like a ghost.
She makes no sound but waits
outside till someone asks her in.

mercado on sunday

6am
stalls ready to roll:
passionfruit
sit in peril
next to prickly *guanábanas*
and honey fragrant *piñas*.
starfish *carambolas*,
magenta *pitahayas*,
fat *sandías* cut in half,
fleshy reds exposed.

winter or summer
it's all the same.

by 7am
the market
roars. the streets
become narrow
as the crowd bloats
and the scene swells
with chit-chat,
laughter,
whistling,
music.

kisses land
on cheeks
like flies.
children stray
and gang up in corners
with soccer balls,
stunts, and dirty jokes.

a busker strums
revolutionary songs,
a poet sways,
still drunk from last night.

maría showcases
the latest
shortest
dress designs each week,
glued to her thighs
with tropical mugginess.
she hopes juan
from the vegetable stall
will notice
when his wife's not looking.

gustavo pretends
to arrange coriander
while he sneaks glances
at juan's wife
when juan
busies his eyes with maría.

there's squabbling,
there's whistling,
there's baskets full
of a whole week's meals.
there's bargaining
for fruit,
for greens,
for time.
11am
the crowd thins,
kisses land
on cheeks

like flies.
'hasta luego,
hasta el próximo
domingo.'
till next week,
next time.

*

july
8am
in the sunday market,
still stars in the sky.
my scarf's
to my nostrils,
my hat's
to my eyelids,
yet the ice in the air
freezes my cheekbones.

a modest crowd
goes about their business.
it's mostly silent –
the only song
is a steady ruffle
of plastic bags
resisting the wind,
the busker
not quite ready
to start
his usual
beatles line up.

winter produce
isn't much.

a variety of greens,
an array of apples,
oranges, carrots,
and lemons,
onions, potatoes.
pale, hard tomatoes
$12.80 the kilo,
stone-hard avocados
$6.50 each.
my nose,
an open faucet,
my now-drenched scarf.

too fast
I settle on one stall,
choose roughly
a whole week's worth
of vegetables and fruit.
i wait in queue and jog in place
to keep the blood flowing.

'thirty-three dollars, seventy cents'
says the chinese woman,
her accent thicker than molasses,
her accounting impeccable.
i scurry to count bills and coins.
'twenty-nine dollars and fifty cents'
i offer, my bargaining skills
corroded from disuse.

she nods
and removes
an orange
and two apples
from my bag.

To whom it may concern

Medical Certificate

This is to certify that the patient seen today (DOB 5/02/2001), from refugee-background and originally from Colombia, has been diagnosed with Adjustment Disorder and stress secondary to this. I believe she has been in New Zealand for three years now, and her irregular attendance at school reflects the overwhelming stress levels she is encountering.

I strongly recommend that she gets regular counselling. Considering convenience and compliance issues, she is most likely to benefit from counselling services at her school. It may also motivate her to attend more regularly if support services are in place to help her communicate with teachers, as well as with fellow students. Perhaps a teacher aide who speaks Spanish?

Please contact me if you have any concerns or queries.
Regards,
Dr J O'Connor

Free delivery

Their empty trolley rattles over potholes.
The morning market's closed and all their crop
of coriander, radish, cress, is sold.
They move slowly. Their feet and ankles ache.

He pushes the trolley, one hand in his pocket,
then changes hands, flexing his cold knuckles.
Trees scatter leaves onto the footpath.
The wind flicks her scarf over her face.

At the far end of the street they see their gate,
the tin letter box, a wall of flowers.
They only allow flowers at the front –
the back is planted every inch to sell.

The children come crowding along the footpath,
their language clattering loudly in its strangeness.
One boy slaps the trolley and calls out.
The couple keep their eyes fixed on the ground.

The boy grabs the handle, clamps his hands
and runs, riding the trolley like a scooter.
He does a graunching wheelie. 'There you go!'
he yells at them, and skids it to their gate.

temporary

she tells them
she'll go back home
one day.
this is temporary
so it doesn't matter
where they send her.

she tells them
she's never been
on a plane.
she can't even recognise
her country's silhouette
on a map.

they give her
a place to go,
a ticket,
a date.

she tells them
she has no bags to pack.
she's carrying all she's got.

she looks
for this place
on the broken screen
of a friend's mobile.
it's hard to find
on the cliff
at the end
of the world.

she boards the flight,
thinks three hours

or maybe four.
one day later,
she's still on it.

she thinks too much
during that time
in the sky
of her children's graves –
one thirteen, one eight –
of her mother
and father
hostage to the farmland
where they were born.

she thinks of the day
she'll go back home,
what she'll wear
and what she'll bring.
she promised
she'd find work fast
to send them money.

she thinks of god
but not too much.
she's still quite upset
at him.

she thinks of the heliconias
in her garden,
the orange and lemon trees.

she falls asleep
and dreams
of landing
in the same place
she just left.

Zimbabwe conversation

'How long?'
'Four years.'
'You've been waiting
four years?'

This country opened its door
a slit and let you through
then slammed it.
Your wife and kids still
on the other side.

'My daughter was six,
now she is ten.
My son was twelve,
now he's sixteen,
almost a man.
Will they still know me?

My wife won't believe me.
She says, "You're not trying."
I'm crazy with trying.

Do you know what
Immigration says?
Your application is in process
Your application is in process
Your application is in process
Your application is in process

Four years of process and no progress.'

Next year

Mr Patel
sits in the corner of our corner shop
between the heater and the cigarettes.
He wears a purple bush shirt and green socks,
on winter nights his knuckles turn to grey.
Every year he rubs his hands and says
'I'm going back to India next year.'

Last week two men came to his shop quite late.
They beat him round the head and took the cash.

Mr Patel
sits in the shop below a new alarm
with red lights winking right across his forehead.
He rubs his hands and says 'I'm going back
to India

next year.'

cha-cha-chá

he's googled the hell out of all colombian music: from *cumbia* to *vallenato* to *bambuco*. he's taken notes on each and every imaginable genre. he's even learned a few dance moves here and there from watching so many videos online.

it's been seven weeks and two days (exactly) since her first day at school. he's counting them.

she's only two desks to his right but he often feels she's galaxies away. her eyes glued to the window, her headphones glued to her ears, his eyes glued to her silky brown hair tied back in a messy ponytail. she wears the uniform in a different way.

'what do you mean, in a different way?' his older brother mocked.
'different uniform to other girls?'
no. same uniform, different way.
'you're smitten with her. you're so smitten with her!'
so what if he is.
'make friends with her friends' his brother suggested. 'easy.'
except she doesn't have friends.
'ask her something – anything' his brother continued.
except he doesn't know two words of spanish.
'ask her what she listens to on her headphones all day.'
bingo.

today is the day.
the bell rings announcing lunch break. she stands up. he knocks back his chair in his anxious frenzy. she looks over her shoulder – at him. she's looking at him.
he freezes.
she pulls off her headphones, takes a step toward him and reaches out.
'help?' she asks, her accent like molasses. he's a fly in the thick of it.
'thanks' he mumbles.

she helps with the chair. he's motionless.

she turns away and he yelps: 'hey, wait. music – who do you like best? juanes? shakira? carlos vives?'

he holds his breath. the next few seconds last an eternity. he's ready to say 'forget it' when she offers 'music? you like colombian music?'

strike while it's hot – he shrugs. 'do you like *vallenato*?'

she smiles. 'no. *lo odio.*'

... come again? *lo*-what?

she turns to leave – 'wait' he says. 'what about *cumbia*?'

her smile widens. '*peor.*'

peor? he rattles his brain. he can't seem to find that genre in his newly-installed music hard drive.

'k-pop' she says. 'i like k-pop.'

k-what?

he's lost in high seas.

'k-pop' she repeats. 'k-pop. from south korea.'

she takes the wishbone wires from her hands and offers him one of the buds.

Conversations

moi

You are teaching me
the numbers for this poem.
moi pi bai buwen
I am tripping and stumbling
on the edges of the sounds
then I lose one small word
altogether. You pick it up,
gently pass it back.

moi pi bai buwen
one two three four
Did I hand those words of ours
as carefully, to you?

pi
Tell me Houmpheng
what did you bring with you?

Only the Buddha.
We came empty-handed,
stripped naked
of all that defines us.

But the Buddha was with us
for hundreds of years.
We carry that knowledge,
fragile and strong,
buried within us.
In that place or this place
no one can take it.

bai
What did you first notice
when you came here?

I noticed that the front doors
were all shut.

buwen
Some of us are looking at the moon.

I say, The moon is made of cheese
and there's an old man
eating his way through it.

Phoeun says, There is a woman
planting rice up there.
Look, do you see her hair
behind her shoulder?
Khim the next says, No,
the shadow in the circle is a tree.
It's where the Buddha sat
and knew the light.

Loeuth, the last, is listening,
then he tells the old words of a poem.
A girl and boy in love,
but she is of a lower birth than he
and so they cannot marry.
The poet says she's like a rabbit
playing in the moonlight
that will never touch the moon.

Look, can't you see the rabbit?

A woman planting rice, a tree,
a girl in love. And cheese.

prum
What is a refugee?

I am a refugee.

No. We offered you refuge, citizenship, a
passport. Those things say you are not a
refugee·

I am a refugee. I wear a second-hand coat.
When it wears out, you give me another second-
hand coat. If I buy a new coat, you say, What
are you doing in that new coat? Don't you know
you're a refugee?

Do you see who I am? I am the child of my
grand-parents, my parents, I have lived with the
monks, I have studied literature, I speak many
languages. I have survived a war. Now I am a
refugee. A refugee is a very small and flat thing.
When will you take your foot off me, so that I
can stand up and be myself again?

prumoi
Here is a small conversation
from Hao Huor and me.

I said, What are you doing, Hao Huor?
(She was scraping the pot
we had used for cooking the rice).
She said, I am putting this rice
outside for the birds.
But birds don't eat rice, I said.
She looked at me. What do they eat?
They eat bread.

Later, I looked.
They had left the bread
and eaten the rice instead.

prumpi
Today you may meet your *kupreng*.

What is *kupreng*?

Kupreng is the love of your life.
The one fate has marked for you
or kept for you from an earlier life.

How do you meet this *kupreng*?

Sometimes you make a small boat,
put in a flower, and set it to drift
on the river. The flower will find her.
Sometimes you sense a direction,
a catch in the wind.

But *kupreng* often comes unexpected·

Will you find your *kupreng*?

I have already met her.

Where is she?

She's dead.

prumbai
Sometimes we sit and say nothing.
Sometimes there's nothing to say.

prumbuwen
What about dying?

Sarouen lets his hands
fall loosely on his knees.
Then he says,
I was in hospital
and I was dying.
All the rest were
dying too, or dead.
So what? He shrugs.

He is a thin black line
on empty paper,
moving casually
towards the margin.

the last
I tell the numbers back to you
moi pi bai buwen
I can't use these words, I say,
I cannot trust myself
on this new ground.
Someone might laugh at me.

You look at me.
You sit there silent.
That is your way of saying
everything.

The BP station

Rain spits on the roof
of Josip's taxi.
There's free parking
if he buys a coffee.
He spreads the newspaper
in front of him.

'I read it every day' he says,
'to remind myself
that I am
an educated man.'

refugee

the teacher greets me
at the classroom door.
'thank you' she says,
'for helping support our – '
she interrupts herself,
looks over her shoulder,
covers her mouth,
whispers
'refugee students.'

i peer over her shoulder
but see only
a handful
of teenagers.

'is being a refugee
a secret?'
i ask,
joking mostly
but kind of not.

she hushes me.
'please, please –
they might hear you
and i'd hate
to offend them.'

offend them.
who does she think
refugees are?

on the whiteboard:
welcome!
miguel from columbia,
makwei from africa.

i worry –
not about miguel
or makwei,
but about the others
in the room.

will they leave
whispering 'refugee' –
thinking columbia and africa
are countries?

Terrorists

'They're all terrorists
over there. They hate the West.'

'Let me tell you this story.

We'd lost our way
on a road that narrowed
into a single lane.
On both sides it was walled
by grass, elbow-high, and yellow flowers.
We were boxed in.
A mob of sheep came crowding through,
rubbing their mangy flanks along our car.
The boy herding them was on a bike
too small for him, his skinny knees
sticking out like wrenches.
I opened the window to ask him
where this dwindling road would take us
but he pulled his checked scarf
across his mouth, saying nothing.
Then he yelled, and charged at the sheep
hustling them furiously past the car
and suddenly he was at our window
staring at these foreigners
stealing his road.

I waited for the graunch
of a handlebar on paint.

He reached into the grass, ripped off a flower
and flung it through the window.'

To Dr J O'Connor

Dear Dr O'Connor,

Thank you for your letter and concern.

At present, we don't have Columbian speakers who can assist with interpreting during counselling sessions. We have submitted an application to the Ministry of Education for funds to cover the expense of having a teacher aide of Columbian background assist with interpreting in counselling as well as during class time.

If the student's attendance does not improve and she continues to miss school, we will have to get in touch with Truancy Services and meet with her parents. Our school cannot make exceptions as all students must follow New Zealand's attendance policy.

Best regards
Michael Smyth
College Counsellor

kitchen

staccato
rolling spanish r's
full of red lipstick
bounce
against the kitchen walls
as this voice
topples over
that voice and
that voice
topples over
all voices.

they make coffee
but coffee is not
what they came for.
it's the brewing.

air gusts
like exhaust
from their mouths.
they keep their coats on.
the southerly
seeps through the cracks
of the weatherboards.
the olive oil's frozen
on the kitchen bench top.

three of them meet
though there could well
be a hundred.
'did you hear about ana
and the english teacher?'
'he's gay!'

'he's not – he's married.'
'married?'
'wait – which ana?
ana sofía?
or ana maría?'
'ana maría –
but did you hear
about ana sofía?'
'she's pregnant.'
'how do you know?!'
'wait –
are you talking about
ana sofía from ascot park
or ana sofía from moera?'
'pregnant? she's got four kids
and no husband –
who's the father?'
'he's white –
the father's white.'
'a *gringo*?
but she doesn't speak
three words of english!'
'who said
you need english
to make babies?'

the coffee's ready
and there's a pack
of vanilla biscuits
but they're all
on a diet.

*

we sit at the dinner table,
the family and me.
we're having silence
with roast lamb and peas.

'pity about the weather'
the mother says
between mouthfuls.
'feels like we barely
had a summer this year.'
'but not too cold today'
the father replies.
'northerly wind gusts
but quite mild.'

the cutlery
bangs and clunks,
a little orchestra
with a far more interesting
conversation.

'we have an intake next week'
i offer.
'thirty-four colombians
being resettled
in this region.'

they raise their eyebrows.
'well'
says the mother,
'let's hope
it doesn't rain.'

Not talking

Two glasses for mint tea, as always,
bread, and a small bowl of dates.
You pour the tea,
hiding the shake in your hand
so I ignore it. You are sitting stiffly.
I know your neck bothers you
but you don't say, and I don't ask.
Nothing is changed. The same postcard
is propped beside the clock.

'Look at that boat' you say
in that blurred accent
you've never lost,
and we watch it
making an unusually
wide sweep of the bay.
'They're searching' I say
and we stare, mesmerised
by this unfolding drama
of something or someone lost.
We breathe easier.

christmas

5.12am on christmas day.
the wind howled all night.
the radio speaks
of gusts and knots,
no mention of jesus
or the holy ghost,
no amen or prayer
she can join in.

there is no wind
where she comes from,
no weather to speak of.
she doesn't understand
the predicament
of knots.

she thinks of christmas eve,
of christmas day
in nariño –
nativity scenes,
the long-winded mass,
piles of cheap presents
wrapped for the children
to tear apart,
glasses of cheap wine,
aguardiente and
eggnog with rum,
the bony pine tree
toppling over with
homemade ornaments
covered in glitter,
and christmas lights
flickering day and night.

all over the top.
too much music
too much food
too much drink
too much talk
too busy
too charged
with celebration.

here in the southern hemisphere,
there is too much silence.

the only lights
she can see
are distant
lamp posts.

here
it is summer.
the days are
too long
too bright
for christmas lights.

the wind picks up,
the radio still on
but no amen plays.

Bread

In the early morning
I walk to the store
to buy some bread.
I pass a car covered in dew,
a dog sleeping on a driveway,
a man pulling open a curtain.

She tells me that in Damascus
buying bread is simple too.

Join the queue outside the shop
pay the money get the bread
pay the money get the bread
fast. Everything is fast.
But not fast enough.
A bomb drops, onto the queue.

She says,
'If you go out to buy some bread
you might not come back.'

Journeys

In 1921, you say, your grandfather
joined the Communist Party.
His mentor was Mao Tse Tung.
In 1922 he was sent to Hong Kong
to bring down the British. He failed
and was imprisoned.

My great-grandfather
sailed from England to New Zealand.
He was twenty years old, never went back,
drowned in a shipwreck off Otago.

Ever the philosopher, you say,
'We never know the endpoint of a journey.
Another coffee?' I nod.
'So tell me about your father.'

lunchtime

he unfolds the tea towel
as though it were
a silk origami.

in it lie huddled
a troupe of *mantu:*
onion and ground beef
in taut steamed dough.
his mouth waters
as he sinks his teeth
into one plump parcel.

the last time
his family shared *mantu*
was the night
before they left kabul.
'to new beginnings'
his mother had said
as they ate
in silence.

he was just a boy.

nine years
in pakistan
with little food.
he and his eight
brothers and sisters
worked twelve hours a day
in whatever
they could.
their parents
worked twelve hours a day,
and twelve hours a night.

then new zealand came
tucked in a big brown envelope
and everything changed.

he is twenty-one
(his mother thinks,
for in afghanistan
they don't have
birthdays).
today
is his first day of school.
his mother was up at dawn
making him *mantu*
for lunch.
'to new beginnings'
she says.

he relishes
the taste,
the care,
and then
'hey you, you're new.'
two boys and a girl
sit by his side.
he smiles and shrugs.
his english isn't good.
'you're too old for school'
one says.
he looks down,
just two *mantu* left.

he offers them
all the same.

boat

cook strait
the night is still.
it's hard to tell
where the ocean ends
and the skies begin.
as if in a dream
the night-shift ferry
glides into view,
a small contained carnival
of glittering lights,
a private celebration.

java sea
he is perched on a slab
on the fishing boat.

he's lost count
of the hours at sea
since his last meal,
since his last drink.
five thousand dollars
bought him the promise
of a boat, 'forty max.'
in the furtive boarding
he'd counted 300
ahead, 100 behind.

the night is still.
it's hard to tell
where the ocean ends
and the skies begin.
heavy with hope
the boat starts to sink

in slow motion
as if in a dream.
the moans and creaks
of boards become high-pitched,
as planks disassemble.

he is perched
on the slab.
it is so tight
he cannot move,
they cannot move.
so many prayers
to so many gods
must have attracted
the devil's attention.

The train

Waikanae to Wellington
'Let's catch the train' I say.
It's almost empty. Mid-morning
and the first rush is over.
We toss our bags carelessly
on the floor. We'll read, or maybe sleep.

Sofia to Belgrade
Milena warned us,
'If you catch the train
it'll be full of refugees.
You have to stay together,
always keep your hands
on your luggage, don't sleep.
Be prepared – at the border
the police will search the train.
It takes a long time
to search a train.'

'Don't catch the train'
Milena said.
'Catch the bus.
Searching a bus is quicker.'

Stones

I skip five flat stones
across the water
the way my father taught me
on this beach when I was six.

I still come every summer.

After you buried your father and
before you boarded the plane in Baghdad,
you threw seven stones over your shoulder
to say that you
were never going back.

withdrawal

they're told
the benefit money
comes to their bank accounts
on wednesdays
by midday.

at 1pm every wednesday
they queue at the atm
and withdraw it all,
look over their shoulders,
stuff the notes in their pockets,
look over their shoulders again
and leave.

they're afraid.

they're afraid the government
will take what's left –
although there's never
anything left.
not one single cent.

they're told:
no one can access
your bank accounts.
not the government,
not work and income.
no one can see
how much money comes in,
no one can see
how much money goes out.
bank accounts in this country
are a private matter.

they nod,
smile,
and queue on wednesday
again.

Pauatahanui Inlet meets South Sudan

The tide is in. It laps the concrete steps
and flows ankle deep across the mud flats.
Abdalla plants his black feet in the
hostile water, and glares at the kayak
I am holding steady.
He sets one foot in it, hauls in the other,
the kayak tilts and throws him on the seat.
His hands grasp the white pole of the paddle.
He dips it, feels the kayak move,
and sees the water slipping past
no deeper than his arm. He will not drown.
He laughs at this plastic thing
that can defeat the sea. He laughs again.

The tide is out. The mud flats stretch
from concrete steps to the distant sea edge.
He stands quite still. He stares in horror.
'Where's all the water gone?' he shouts.

plate

people
unknown
greet him
at the airport
with smiles
and signs
that say
'welcome'
in his language.

they show him
how to catch a bus,
where the shops
and his english classes are.
they give him
blankets,
a torch
and a book
he cannot read,
some clothes
for winter
though none
that fit.

they invite him
for dinner.
'bring a plate'
they say.
so he goes
to the second-hand shops and gets
the nicest china plate
he can afford.

arrested development

he sits
in front of the tv
or the computer.

he sits
on the bus,
or in his english class.
and feels
the calluses on his hands
grow thin.

he sits
while he explains
he wants –
he needs –
to find a job.
he's going insane
at home.
not enough english,
they say
again and again

he sits
while she says
'*vagabundo*,
i should never have married you,'
while she tells
their three daughters
'your father's a good-for-nothing.
he can't even afford
to get you *princesas*
good new clothes.'

he sits
and rubs his temples
at lunchtime
at dinnertime
when he can't eat,
at 3am
when he can't sleep.

he sits
at work and income.
he asks the interpreter
to please tell
the gentleman behind the desk
he's never hit her
but feels he will
any moment now.
he's losing it.
she's driving him mad –
he's going mad.
they're going mad.

he asks,
can they please
support him
in some way?
can he get
accommodation elsewhere
for a few nights –
to cool off,
think things over?
he's afraid he'll flip
and come crashing
against her.
he's embarrassed
about asking

but what's he to do?
who's he to trust?

no.
he can't get support.
'you need a police report
showing proof
of domestic violence.'

he needs to hit his wife,
be arrested
and then,
maybe,
he can receive an allowance
for one night
away from home.

he needs to hit her first?

he sits
and listens,
in disbelief.

he stands up.
he walks away.

Naming

'Pardon?'

'Senanayake Mudiyanselage Devinda Danushka Bandara Senanayake.'

'Um ... Sena ... Can you spell it?'

'S-e-n-a-n-a-y-a-k-e M-u-d ...'

'No no no, that's enough. What do I call you? Sennie?'

'No, Devinda.'

'Devinda! Why didn't you put that first then?'

'Because my names have a different order. And they all mean something. Senanayake means the leader of a legion. Mudiyanse means a rank, like lieutenant or captain, and lage means to belong. Like, the lieutenant that belongs to the leader.'

'You can't be the leader and the lieutenant at the same time. That's rubbish. What about the others?'

'I don't know what Bandara means. Danushka means the archer.'

'Archer? Bow and arrow archer?'

'Yep.'

'Weird. What about Devinda?'

'Devinda is the name of the head god.'

'So you're the head god, you're the leader, you're the lieutenant, and you're the foot soldier – well, the archer. You're a whole army all in one. Whoo! But I'm going to call you Sennie. That's okay, isn't it.'

'Fine. What do I call you?'

'Hugh. H-u-g-h. Hugh. Get an easy name like that.'

underwater

i'm sixteen.
'head west'
father said
and forbade me to look back
over my shoulder.
i think of sodom and lot,
of his wife,
and their fate.
the sun blasts
on to my neck.
i walk,
i do not stop.

ten thousand steps
and i arrive
at the camp,
blistered bones,
a numb soul.
there is no rest
in the july heat
of east sudan,
for in hell,
not even the devil sleeps.

no running water.
the stench
is oppressive.
i pretend
i'm underwater
and i learn
to hold
my breath.

ten thousand miles
and i arrive
at the end of the world.
it is july
and all is cold.
the wind howls
its welcome
in a language
i do not know.

i have a roof,
food,
running water.
i have everything
i need
except that they forget
the blankets
for the bed.
its steel frame
touches my skin,
freezes my feet –
i'm too long,
too brown,
i do not fit.

what you grow used to

a mother
gives birth to twins,
delivers the placenta,
walks away,
leaves her babies
behind.

thirty-five people
die in a day,
the stench of death
on your clothes,
on your hair,
in your pores.
you count
the daily tally of corpses
piled next to the river.

the cries of children
become white noise –
like the steady hum
of the refrigerator
you once had.

you're so tired
you have
dreamless sleep.
it is only
when you wake up
that the nightmares begin.
but you grow used
to them as well.
there are too many
to tell where one ends
and the next begins.

the ticket out
finally comes.
you've never heard
of the country
but you arrive.

here,
days are peaceful,
nights are quiet.
people are pleasant,
streets have green and red men
to show
when it's safe
to cross.

people pick up after their dogs.
you read somewhere
they get fined
if they don't.

here,
you have a house,
a flushing toilet,
hot water.

here,
silence is oppressive:
you can't sleep.

here,
you realise
you left
the camp
but the camp
never leaves you.

medicine

to whom it may concern:

i'm sick today and i won't be at school again.

when we lived in colombia, i loved school. i used to have the best
grades. then we had to move to ecuador. that wasn't too bad because i
used to be the best student there as well. some kids liked me because
i'd help them with their homework. other kids didn't. they were
jealous.

here, nobody likes me. here, nobody speaks my language. they can't
say my name. they can't spell my country.

when the alarm goes off at ten past six, it feels like water flooding
– first my head, then my body. when i'm in school, my head spins.
sometimes the classroom spins. my eyes itch and burn. i feel pain in
my neck, my shoulders, my back. i study and pay attention then the
throbbing in my head takes over and i forget all i've learned.

every day is like starting again.

i want to love school like i did before. i want to understand the
teacher and my classmates. i want to raise my hand and have answers
to questions. i want to laugh and have friends. i want to learn english
so i can understand them and they can understand me.

but today i'll stay home. my head hurts too much, i can't even see.

i don't know what you call this illness. i don't know if there's a cure for
it at all.

sincerely,
laura alejandra

Postmark

The envelope is face down
on the table.

Prak's first wife has been found.
She's been lost for twenty years,
in the war, in the countryside.
She cannot read or write,
she cannot scan down lists or read papers.
Now she is found, and she has found him.
She wants to come. She begs to come.

He has a new wife, a teenage son,
a small house by the sea.
His new wife reads and writes
and has many friends on Facebook.
His son wants to work in IT.

A tide is rising, threatening to engulf him.
He wants to throw the envelope in the sea.

Ashes

Alika climbs onto a chair and lifts
the cups and saucers with pink roses
from the top shelf of the highest cupboard.
She pours one cup for me, and one for her
then lays a row of photographs between.

Her mother has just died in Laos.
A pink and orange canopy
sways on a bamboo raft.
The poles bite the shoulders
of the men. They walk through
green rice fields, on a brown track.
The monks in orange robes have umbrellas.
A small boy holds up a bowl of eggs.

Her son is watching cartoons on TV.
He never met his grandmother.

Now they are burning the body.
Smoke drifts through tall bamboo,
her sisters are grey silhouettes.

A truck grinds past the open window,
there's the black smell of exhaust.
She bangs the window shut and sighs,
a long breath of exile.

I push my chair back, stand to leave,
she pulls her son onto his feet.
'Say good bye.' He grunts, his eyes
swiveling back to the screen.

shangri-la

'bhutan! you're from bhutan! the happiest place on earth! the one and only shangri-la – wow. i've never met anyone from bhutan' he says.

'but i've read all about your gross national happiness' he continues. 'that's what i call progress: economy in terms of citizens' wellbeing. impressive.'

no. i want to say: no. bhutan is not the happiest place on earth. instead i smile, so as to avoid being rude. he mistakes it for modesty.

i don't tell him my three daughters, my wife, her mother, and i have been refugees from bhutan for more than 20 years.

i don't tell him we are *lhotshampas* – he wouldn't know about *lhotshampas*. few people do. we never made headlines.

i don't tell him bhutan is the world's biggest creator of refugees per capita. nearly 100,000 people of nepalese origin were expelled in the 1990s, us among them. one-sixth of bhutan's population.

i don't tell him our national slogan 'one nation, one people' leaves no margin for difference.

i don't tell him there is little room for happiness in a country ruled by an absolute monarchy.

i keep quiet and let him feel proud for sharing what he thinks he knows about bhutan. because in bhutan i learned that people don't like being contradicted. they don't like being told they are wrong.

Towards Iraq

The southerly is blowing across the graves.
As Akram walks on the wet grass
his foot slips. The coins in his hand
scatter. They lie like the stones
he threw behind him when he left.
He is silent, perhaps waiting
for a bell to toll or for mourners to weep
for all his loss.

The grave faces east – not where God is
but where home is – and weeds he's never seen
are already creeping out from under the granite.

Eyewitness, Java

I see the sky blazing with fire,
I see the silhouette of the volcano,
the air filling with choking ash,
then rain falling. I see that rain
falling on the loose warm
face of the smoking mountain,
falling on trees, roofs, the river
surface pitted with it. I see roads
beginning to run awash,
the river creeping up the banks.
I see her at her door, anxious,
the land so heavy now with water,
then I hear it, the thunderous noise,
the still-loose mountain breaking apart,
rock and mud tearing down
across rice fields, dragon trees,
houses with tile roofs, concrete yards,
all swept up in this monstrous wave
driving forward, and then,
inexplicably, turning a fraction,
and looping right around her house.

I see her staring in disbelief.

She is sitting beside me,
her scarf slipping back off her head,
her skirt the colour of brown mud,
telling me in her pieces of English,
her wild hands flying, her words painting
picture after picture,
chaos and loss,
making me an eye witness too.

The great voyagers

All the great voyagers return
Homeward as on an arc of thought.

On the Foxton stop bank
a dog is running off the lead.
He rushes furiously,
barking, ears flattened,
away from his owner
who walks evenly,
saying nothing.
And suddenly
the dog rushes back.

Those first Jansens never once
went home to Denmark.
Landed at Foxton – a wharf,
maybe a shop, some horses,
and that was it.
Bundled themselves over the Rimutakas
to hard labour in a tough new land.
But maybe, of an evening, an arc of thought
slipped away over the curve of the world
to touch on a village, maybe footprints
in the snow, maybe boots outside a door,
maybe a fireplace, maybe a table,
maybe a plate of codfish.
Or maybe that arc of thought looped lightly
over that village, over that table
then drifted back on the long curve,
to this new land
slowly becoming home.

Acknowledgements

Some of Adrienne's poems previously appeared in: *The 4th Floor*, *Landfall, a stone seat and a shadow tree*, and *Keel & Drift*.

The epigraph at the beginning of the poem, 'The great voyagers', is reproduced from 'The Homecoming' in Howes, Barbara. 1954. *In the Cold Country*. New York: Bonacio & Saul/Grove Press.

A big thank you to:
Lynn Jenner, for reading these poems with wisdom and perceptiveness.

Whitireia New Zealand, for generously supporting this publication.

Wes Hollis and Devinda Danushka, for all their behind-the-scenes work with Landing Press.

The publishing team from the Whitireia New Zealand publishing programme – Samantha Guillen, Katrina Fankhauser, Telford Mills, Vanessa Ward, Rebecca Chester, Hannah Robson, Allie Davis, and Alex Stronach, and their tutors Helen Heath and Marie Hodgkinson, for all their work in the production and promotion of this book.

The poems by writer

by Adrienne

Lost in translation; Writing in Arabic; Mary; The English class;
Free delivery; Zimbabwe conversation; Next year; Conversations;
The BP station; Terrorists; Not talking; Bread; Journeys; The train;
Stones; Pauatahanui Inlet meets South Sudan; Naming; Postmark;
Ashes; Towards Iraq; Eyewitness, Java; The great voyagers

by carina

all of us; homework; read; english; hearing aid; mercado on
sunday; To whom it may concern; temporary; cha-cha-chá;
refugee; To Dr J O'Connor; kitchen; christmas; lunchtime; boat;
withdrawal; plate; arrested development; underwater; what you
grow used to; medicine; shangri-la

For most of her life Adrienne Jansen has been writing alongside migrants to New Zealand to tell their stories – in fiction, non-fiction, and now in poetry. 'Personal stories have the power to shift our heads,' she says. She lives in Porirua with her family.

carina gallegos has a background in journalism and development studies. originally from costa rica, she moved to new zealand thirteen years ago and has worked with refugee-background communities since 2011. she lives in wellington with her family.

Also from Landing Press

Trish Harris's first collection of poetry is a poetic memoir of a long stay in hospital. On this poignant journey through the swells and up draughts of recovery, hope and humour are never far away.

In these poems by Adrienne Jansen, a girl carries a tray of eggs on her fingertips, a man plays a cello in a field, a woman buys a carpet sweeper – these moments of everyday life are deceptively simple. Underneath, something else is going on – a sense of mystery, an awareness of impending death, a wry view of human nature.

Landing Press
Available from bookshops and
landingpress.wordpress.com